YESTERDAY'S TRADES

YESTERDAY'S TRADES

Molly Perham

ABELARD-SCHUMAN: LONDON

ISBN 0 200 71927 0

Printed in Great Britain

LONDON
Abelard-Schuman Limited
158 Buckingham Palace Road,
London SW1

24 Market Square,
Aylesbury, Bucks.

Contents

Introduction

This is the second title of a new series of books aimed at using various kinds of contemporary source material to show social life in Britain through the ages.

The number of trades and crafts is endless, and I have only been able to choose about a dozen. However, I have made my selection as varied as possible, and interested readers can do just as I have done with crafts of their own choosing.

The chapters in between about folklore, surnames, child labour and so on, are intended to give a broader background to the subject.

I hope that this method of learning history is stimulating to the reader. The aim is to provide basic information and encourage readers to find out more for themselves. This way the knowledge is far more likely to stick, than if you just read it all in a book.

I have included a list of museums at the back of the book. Any subject is made more interesting when you can actually *see* something. And there are many suggestions of things to do in the text.

Molly Perham

1. The Wool Trade

Though Jason's Fleece was fam'd of old,
The British wool is growing gold;
No mines can more of wealth supply,
It keeps the peasants from the cold,
And takes for Kings the Tyrian dye.
Dryden, from 'King Arthur'

Dryden's boast about British wool 'growing gold' is more than true. For seven hundred years from the twelfth to the nineteenth century it was our most important industry. During the reign of William III the wool trade accounted for two-thirds of British exports, and Englishmen proudly boasted that we 'clothed half of Europe by our English cloth.' It was so important that the Lord Chancellor's seat is stuffed with it even today.

What is the name of his seat?

The wool trade provided work for many different craftsmen. If your surname is Dyer, Fuller, Lister, Tucker, Walker or Webster you can be sure that one of your ancestors worked in the trade.

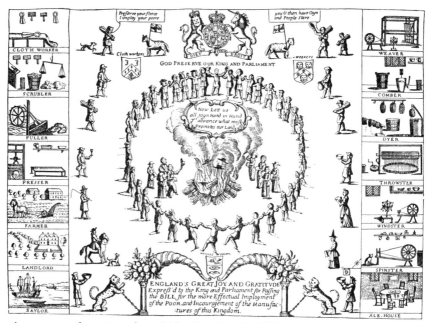

A seventeenth century broadside showing the different processes of the wool trade.

Can you think of any other surnames connected with the wool trade?

What did all these different craftsmen do? A poem by R. Watts printed in 1614 describes all the different processes of cloth-making.

> At first, the Parter, that doth neatly cull
> The Finer from the warser sort of wool.
> The Dyer then in order next doth stand
> With sweating brow and a laborious hand.
> Withal they then asperge it, which being done,
> The careful hand of Mixers round it run.
> The stock-carder his arms doth hard employ
> (Remembering Friday is our Market Day).

The fleece, after the shearing, was sorted into different lengths and qualities by the Parter. Then the Dyer washed and scoured the

Hargreaves' Spinning Jenny. With the old spinning wheel that Hargreaves' wife used, she thinned the thread by pulling it off the distaff by hand. The Spinning Jenny did this with a travelling carriage.

wool to remove the grease, and then dyed it. The Mixer teased the wool into fluff for the Carder, who straightened out the fibres with two hand-cards. These were about twelve inches long and looked like brushes with pieces of wire fitted into them instead of bristles. By the time the wool was stripped from the cards it was in soft fleecy rolls called 'slivers', ready for the spinning wheel.

In 1755 Richard Arkwright invented a machine for carding using revolving rollers, and this, of course, made the work much easier and quicker.

What else did Richard Arkwright invent?

The next process was spinning.

Can you find out what the person who did spinning was called?
What does the word mean today?

Until the fourteenth century spinning was done on a distaff and spindle, then the spinning wheel was invented. Since this could be done at home it was called a 'cottage industry'. Fifteenth-century housewives worked at home making blankets and clothes for their own households as well as extra to sell.

In 1733 James Kay invented the Flying Shuttle, which made weaving so fast that faster spinning was needed to keep up with the weavers. By 1764 James Hargreaves, a poor weaver, was able to perfect a spinning machine, which kept pace with the weavers, after watching his wife at work. He called it his Spinning Jenny. Another inventor, Samuel Crompton, made an even better machine which is still in use today. It has an unusual name.

Do you know what it is?

Weaving is the process of making the spun thread into cloth by using a shuttle which darts in and out of straight threads going in the opposite direction. It is a bit like darning. The threads are called warp and weft.

12

Samuel Crompton improved Hargreaves' and Arkwright's machines, and invented this machine in 1774.

Do you know which is which?

For many years weaving was done by throwing the shuttle from one hand to the other, then James Kay invented the 'Flying' Shuttle, which doubled the speed at which the weaver could work. The first power loom, driven by steam-engines, was made by the Reverend Edmund Cartwright at the end of the eighteenth century.

There were still several jobs to do before the woven cloth was ready for the market. The Brayer scoured out any dirt or oil; the Burler picked out the knots, then it was fulled. Fulling meant soaping the cloth and then beating it with heavy wooden hammers

13

A fulling machine. The 'stocks' rise and fall while the trough is moved backwards and forwards.

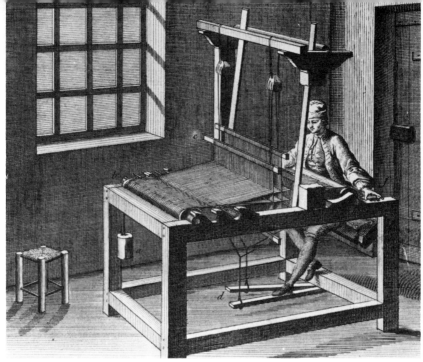

There are still some handlooms at work today, but in the eighteenth century the weaver worked at home on a hand loom.

Spinning and weaving were 'cottage industries' in the eighteenth and early nineteenth centuries and almost every country cottage would have its own spinning wheel.

A modern spinning frame—a vast improvement on the old spinning wheel!

until it looked like felt. Originally it used to be trampled under-
foot, and then the fuller was called a 'walker'. Power driven fulling
machines were invented in the fifteenth century. The finishing
process involved raising the nap and shearing it neatly, and finally
patching up any holes.

What was it like to work in the wool trade in mediaeval times?

Try and get a copy of The Wool Pack *by Cynthia Harnett. This
book captures the atmosphere of fifteenth-century life in the
wool trade, and tells the story of a boy living then.*

In the seventeenth century working hours were long and wages
were low. A weaver would work from four in the morning until
eight, nine or ten o'clock at night for nine or ten shillings a week.
A child who was not earning by the time he was six years old was
called idle. The young children fetched bobbins, wound yarn, and
helped the weaver get his loom ready for work. They didn't earn
much. The small ones were paid a penny a day, rising to fourpence

16

a day when they were twelve. Undernourished, uncared for and often unwanted, the children died like flies, sometimes standing at their looms.

Towards the end of the eighteenth century people began to feel uneasy about the new machines which were being invented. They thought they would take over the work and leave them unemployed. Mobs of men rioted, breaking and burning the hated machinery.

What were the people called who attempted to destroy machines and factories?

But in fact the invention of machines for spinning and weaving meant that large new factories were built which provided more work for more people. Weekly wages rose dramatically, and every family was taking home fifty to a hundred shillings a week.

17

2. The Collier

Did you know that it was only after 1842 that it was forbidden to employ children under the age of ten in the coal mines? Up till then children as young as six years had spent all the hours of daylight working in the pits. They worked in total darkness, sometimes in pools of water, carting coal and assisting the miners. Then, carried home by their parents, frequently asleep, they were taken to their small and often insanitary homes for the night, only to be woken early the following morning for another day's work.

Since the time of Queen Elizabeth I coal-mining had been of importance to this country, and during the Industrial Revolution the supply of coal was essential—and the great industrialists didn't care how they got it. No one cared very much about the people who hacked out the coal. As the pits grew deeper and deeper, the miners spent more and more time far away underground, and became cut off from the rest of the world. Hundreds of workers were killed in explosions which were caused by fire-damp.

What invention made for greater safety in the pits?

*The first mines were 'open cast'. This meant people just dug coal out of the·
surface of the ground. Later deep shafts were dug and coal mining became an
industry.*

During the nineteenth century a number of people began to realise
that the use of child labour was shameful, and they campaigned to
make it illegal. Progress was slow at first, but gradually the cam-
paign gathered momentum and by the end of the nineteenth
century children were no longer regarded as working animals.

*Do you know who brought in the 1842 Mines Act? What did it
say?*

Pit ponies took over the job of carrying coal. These poor ponies
even had their stables underground, so they never saw the light of
day. It is only very recently that the last of the pit ponies was
retired.

At the beginning of the twentieth century people began to be
aware of the appalling conditions in which the men worked. A
great writer, D. H. Lawrence, did much to publicise their working
conditions.

19

Women coal bearers

You will find passages about miners in many of D. H. Lawrence's books. Can you find out why he was interested in them?

Celia Fiennes, a seventeenth-century woman who travelled up and down England on horseback, kept a diary of things that interested her. This was later published in book form as *Through England on a Side Saddle*. In 1697 she described a coal-mine in Derbyshire:

> They make their mines at ye Entrance like a Well and so till they Come to ye Coale then they digg all the Ground about where there in Coale and set pillars to support it, and so bring it to ye well where be a basket Like a hand barrow by Cords they pull it up—so they Let down and up the miners with a Cord . . . they generally look very pale and yellow that work Underground, they are forced to keep lights with them and some tymes are forced to use Gunpowder to break the stones, and that is sometymes hazardous to the people and destroys them at work.

When you have finished this book, why not write a diary of everyday events like Celia Fiennes'?

A visit from the farrier for Shep, the pit pony.

Early twentieth century miners using pick-axes to hack coal from a seam. The pit-props are made of wood.

Nearly a century later in 1782, Thomas Newte reported that miners at Worsley mine earned 20d. to 3 shillings (8p-15p) a day, according to the quantity of coal dug. This was not very much to live on, for at the end of the eighteenth century the price of corn was very high, and bread was 15d. (6p) for a quartern loaf.

How much does a miner earn today? How do you think this compares with the wages of 1782?

The pick-axe was still the main tool, even at the beginning of this century. The men crouched at the coal face, stripped to the waist and wet with perspiration. The longwall method was used. This meant that a section of the coal face, perhaps 100 yards in length, was cut back, and then cut back again, as a continuous operation. Pit-props then were made of wood and there were three dangers always present: falling rocks, floods, and gases from the coal-seam. The hazards of coal-dust were always there too—and this could mean lung trouble as well as the danger of fire.

22

One of the first lifts to be used for getting miners to the coal face.

Do you know the name of the disease which affects miners?

As a result of publicity, a Coal Mines Act was passed in 1911 which made it necessary for all mine owners to provide rescue facilities and first aid equipment for the colliers. Then in 1920 the Miners' Welfare Fund was established. This fund was used to help the dependants of miners who were killed or injured at work, and to build up amenities at the pits. One important aim was to provide baths and changing rooms at the pit-head, so that the men could leave work clean and tidy, instead of going home black.

Miners became politically minded towards the end of the nineteenth century, and helped to build the Labour Party.

What is their trade union called? How many members does it have?

Pneumatic drills are now used instead of pick-axes. The pit-props are much more sophisticated affairs made of steel.

Which Socialist MP did much to further the cause of the miners?

In the late 1930s the coal-mines began to become mechanised. Pneumatic drills are now used instead of pick-axes, and electric or compressed-air cutters are used for getting coal and transporting it to the bottom of the shaft for hoisting to the surface. Today the world's most advanced coal-mine is Bevercotes Colliery, in Nottinghamshire. It has been called 'the pit of the twenty-first century'. From a central control room on the surface all operations in the mine are linked by remote control. Every activity of the mine can be observed, from coal-faces to coal preparation plant. Underground locomotives have a radio link to the control room. A far cry from the days of the child coal bearer!

It has often been said that Britain's power rested on coal. The recent miners' strike did much to show us how many things, both in industry and in our everyday lives, rely on coal.

How many things can you think of that depend on coal? What would life be like without it?

Britain's first remote control pit at Bevercotes Colliery. This underground locomotive is linked by radio to the central control room.

Until 1972 the miners had not been on strike since 1926, when there was a General Strike. After the First World War there was a great deal of unemployment and a shortage of houses. What the returning soldiers found was nothing like the 'Homes Fit For Heroes' which they had been promised. So the three great unions of Miners, Railwaymen, and Transport and General Workers came out on strike. Unfortunately the strike didn't help the workers at all, but contributed to an economic depression which hit the whole country. Families in the industrial areas had a very bleak life in the 1920s and 1930s.

The daughter of an unemployed miner in the 1920's wrote:

> 'Food was largely bread and potatoes. Breakfast was porridge with milk and sugar. Once a week mother queued at the butcher and came home if lucky with two-penny worth of bacon bones, and made pea-soup for the midday meal.'

Life is hard for the unemployed today, but not as bad as it was then.

Do you know how many unemployed people there are today? If you were a member of the Government, what plans would you have for helping the unemployment problem?

25

3. Child Labour

You might well be thankful that you are young in the 1970s and not in the 1770s. Today you have all the benefits of the Welfare State, free education, the National Health Service, and you don't start full time work until you are sixteen, at the earliest.

Childhood as we know it did not exist for children of the lower classes in the eighteenth century. They were sent out to work at about six years of age. In fact some people frowned upon them if they were not making their contribution to society by that time.

Young children worked in the mines dragging trucks of coal to the pit-mouth, or sitting all day in the dark, opening and shutting trap doors. In the country, boys of seven and eight years worked as bird-scarers in the fields, while small girls helped their mothers to make lace, or knit gloves and stockings at home.

Factories employed children along with their parents, and they often worked up to twelve or fifteen hours a day. The new machines did not need much physical strength, and the factory owners did not want to pay a man for what a child could do. A

26

Children carrying clay in the brickyards.

man called John Aikin wrote about child workers in the cotton mills in 1795. He said:

> 'These children are usually too long confined to work in close rooms, often during the whole night: the air they breathe from the oil etc. employed in the machiny is injurious. Little regard is paid to their cleanliness . . .'

A Factory Act was passed in 1802, and another in 1819, which said that no child under the age of nine was to be employed, and those between nine and sixteen must not work more than twelve hours a day. But no one took much notice of these laws because the local magistrate was usually a factory owner himself.

The poorest families sold their little boys to a chimney-sweep

27

Children at work in the coal mines, pushing trucks loaded with coal.

for the sum of twenty or thirty shillings. To be a sweep's climbing-boy was the worst job of all. The sweeps, often rough, dishonest men, hardly bothered to wash and feed the boys, who were always black with soot and in rags. One master would buy as many as twenty-four climbing-boys and hire them out for sixpence a day in the winter. In the summer they were forced to beg in the streets for their food. Often the small boys would have to climb chimneys that were actually on fire. The most profitable part of the sweep's trade was putting out fires in chimneys.

A chimney-sweep of Knightsbridge gave evidence in 1788 that when he was ten years old he was sent up a chimney that had been on fire for forty-eight hours, and that his master came and found fault with him 'in so angry a manner as to occasion a fright, by which means he fell down into the fire and was much burnt and crippled by it for life'.

Charles Kingsley's story, The Water Babies, *is about a climbing-boy called Tom. This book helped to bring to the public's attention the misery of these small boys.*

A man called Thomas Coram wanted to do something to stop the miserable lives of eighteenth-century children. He started the Foundling Hospital for orphans. Before that unwanted children
28

Child labour in the early nineteenth century, spinning yarn in a weaving factory.

Factory children on their way to work.

were put into workhouses, where few of them survived. Those that did were apprenticed to a trade at the age of seven, and the parish funds paid £5 to their master.

If you want to know more about what it was like living in a workhouse, read Oliver Twist *by Charles Dickens.*

It was not until the middle of the nineteenth century that people tried to help these poor children. People like Lord Shaftesbury and Sir Robert Peel brought their misery to the public's attention, and gradually thoughtful people began to realise that a child's early years should be spent in school, not in workshops. Charity schools and Sunday schools did a lot of good work in educating the poor wretches, and in 1870 the Government made education compulsory for every child between five and fourteen years of age.

Today a child's health and education are one of the priorities of the Welfare State.

A sweep's 'climbing boy' in 1853.

Do you know who was responsible for the foundation of the Welfare State? When did it begin?

In June 1945 family allowances were paid for every child after the first. The aim was to make sure every child was well provided for. The weekly payment was five shillings.

Do you know how much the family allowance is today?

4. The Blacksmith

I see the smithy, with its fires aglow,
I hear the bellows blow,
And the shrill hammer on the anvil beat
The iron white with heat.

Longfellow

Longfellow has been called the poet of the forge, as in many of his poems there are references to the blacksmith. In fact he did much to promote the blacksmith as a worthy member of the community.

See how many of Longfellow's poems you can find in which the forge is mentioned. Perhaps you can also find out what inspired him to write these poems.

The blacksmith has always been one of the most important craftsmen of a community, as he was the one who made all the tools used by the other craftsmen. His forge was often a meeting place for the villagers, where they would go to exchange gossip. Many

32

The Blacksmith's forge was an important part of village life.

The Ridgeway Forge on the outskirts of Sheffield is one of the few forges which still work metal by hand, using the ancient methods. In the picture the blacksmith and striker are working on a red hot bar.

people believed the smith had magic powers for curing the sick, and certainly he often acted as a vet. There are many inn signs which show horseshoes or anvils in their design, and this is an indication of how important the blacksmith was.

Have a look at the old inn signs in your district and see how many relate to the blacksmith.

There have been primitive furnaces for heating metal since Roman times. Special hearths were built on a hillside so that the wind fanned the flames and raised the heat of the fire. An Early Bronze Age smith's furnace found in Ireland dates back to about 1800 BC. Remains of the early metal ages have been found in the shape of spears, arrowheads, axes, daggers and swords.

By the thirteenth century the smith had become very important: he made ploughshares and other agricultural equipment as well as weapons of war. These early smithies were open on all four sides, with just a roof above to keep off the rain. Under the feudal

34

A blacksmith working on a hand forged wrought iron gate.

This is a photograph of a silversmith's small hammer being forged from a red hot bar.

system of mediaeval times the blacksmith was a servant of the manor, like most other craftsmen.

What do you know about the Feudal System?

After the Middle Ages the smiths began to specialise: some became armourers, some locksmiths, while others carried on making and repairing tools and shoeing horses.

During the nineteenth century the smith began to lose his importance as an increasing number of engineering works and iron foundries took over his work. He no longer made tools, but still did repairs and farriery (shoeing horses). In Victorian times he was very often the only man in the village with any veterinary skill, and in remote villages he was often asked to cut hair or pull out teeth as well!

When cars began to replace horses in the early 1900s, many blacksmiths opened garages. In 1911 one of them, Stan Merritt, wrote a poem which is a parody of Longfellow's *The Village Blacksmith:*

36

Piercing by hand a St George and the Dragon weather vane.

Beneath a huge electric sign,
The village smith now sits,
His brawny form, though plump and fat,
His easy chair just fits.

The old clay pipe is laid away,
His brow reveals no sweat,
He calmly views the cars roll up
And puffs a cigarette.

Six shiny pumps adorn the spot
Where once the anvil stood.
The heavy traffic daily pays
This modern Robin Hood.

Compare these verses with Longfellow's poem.

Today even horseshoes can be bought ready made, and there are only a few traditional smithies left in rural areas. Even these will probably use power drills and an oxy-acetylene plant along with the traditional blacksmith's tools.

If you have a blacksmith in your area, do go and watch him work. This is a trade that is almost obsolete, and soon there will be no blacksmiths left. As you step inside the forge, you will probably see nothing at first except the glowing hearth. The hearth is about six feet by four feet and is constructed of brick, with a flue at the back to take away the smoke and fumes. Near the hearth are the bellows and a little shovel called a 'slice' for tending the fire. At the front of the hearth is a tank of water called a 'bosh' for quenching the iron and cooling the tools. On the walls hang a row of tools—swages, flatters and fullers, used for making the iron bars thinner. As well as these the blacksmith will have a variety of tongs, hammers, mandrels, and of course the anvil.

Suppose you have brought a horse to be shod. This part of the blacksmith's work is called farriery. First of all the farrier will examine all the hoofs, fore hoofs first so that the horse is not frightened. When the old shoes have been removed, the hoofs are rasped and picked clean with a buffer and a paring knife. The farrier keeps all his tools for shoeing horses in a special box. Then the new shoes are tried for fit, just like we try on shoes in a shoeshop. If the shoes fit, they are heated and held to the hoof to 'seat'. As this is done you will see clouds of smoke, but there is no need to get alarmed, the hoof is completely insensitive to heat. When the shoe is cold it is nailed on with a small hammer, and the nails are clinched at the points where they stick out. Now the horse is ready for the day's work.

Blacksmiths and farriers have never been well paid. In 1900 you could get a carthorse shod for 3s 6d. (17½p).

See if you can find out how much you would pay for having a horse shod today.

Most of the blacksmith's trade today is in wrought-iron work. The modern smith obtains his iron in bars, but up until the fourteenth century the smiths had to beat out their own bars. It is the un-eveness of the iron that distinguishes very early wrought-iron work.

38

This beautiful hand forged grille depicts the tree of life. The large centre panel shows the original English oak being killed by the parasitic vine. Round the outside border in a clockwise direction are some of the stages of manufacture: mining, blast furnace, water wheel, trip hammer, blacksmith's shop with hearth, anvil and tools. The border then completes the full cycle back to a live oak branch.

See if you can find some wrought-iron work in your town. The church will be a likely place. Do you think it is old or new?

By the eighteenth century the blacksmiths had perfected the art of making scrolls—thin iron bars wound round and round in a spiral—and began to use other patterns in their work. They made all kinds of gates, railings, balconies, fire-irons, brackets, hinges, and chimney cranes.

There is still a Guild of Blacksmiths in the City of London, and their motto is 'By hammer and hand all arts do stand'. When you have seen some of their beautiful wrought-iron work you might well agree with this.

5. The Swordsman

In the late fourteenth century, if you beat your opponent in single combat, his horse, armour and arms were all yours. In those days the armoured knight was worth about £20,000 of today's money, so for the swordsman the stakes were high, though the risks were great.

Swords and sword-fighting conjure up thousands of years of history, legend, romance and fable: enchanted swords, magic swords, and swords whose names are as famous as those of the heroes who owned them. You must have heard about the Sword of Damocles: Damocles was invited to a banquet by Dionysius and found himself seated under a naked sword suspended by a single hair.

How many other legends of heroes and their swords do you know?

As well as their exciting history, swords have a special appeal for many people because they are objects of beauty as well as

A foot soldier of the time of James I, armed with a cavalier.

weapons of war. The variety in pattern and design is what has prevented the craft of the swordsmith from dying with the invention of more modern manufacturing methods. Each country had swords of a different design; no two regiments had exactly identical swords, and soldiers often had their own name, or rank, embossed on the blade.

The most beautiful swords of all are presentation swords. These are not made for use in battle, but are given by a sovereign as a token of respect or gratitude. King George VI presented a sword to the city of Stalingrad; Charlemagne sent one to Egbert, King of Wessex.

To which famous man did the East India Company present a jewelled sword after the victory at Plassey?

The sword has always been a symbol of sovereignty. At British coronations three swords are used, and the Sword of State is carried on all State occasions.

Can you think of any other ceremonies which include a sword?

Swords made by swordsmiths today are either highly decorated presentation swords, or ceremonial weapons. They are still carried by the officers of most of the world's armed forces, but they have been obsolete since the First World War.

Do you know the length of the standard Service blade?

The earliest swords were made of bronze in about 1500 BC. They were either cast in a mould or hammered out of a lump of bronze. After the sword was made it was decorated by hand to suit the customer's wishes. The craft of the swordsmith has not changed much since those days, except of course that the blade is now forged from bar steel by mechanical hammers, instead of by the swordsmith's arm.

The Phoenicians are said to have discovered the properties of bronze. Of what two metals is it an alloy?

43

Sir Thomas Fairfax, Knight General of the Forces raised by Parliament for the Civil War in the seventeenth century. Notice the elaborate hilt of his rapier.

Wilkinson Sword Factory in 1890.

However bronze was not the ideal material for swords, as it was so heavy. So about the first century BC the Roman swordsmiths produce a type of iron sword. The Gauls who sacked Rome in 390 BC had iron swords, but reports of the time say that the swords were so soft that after a hard blow had struck home on the opponent's shield, the swordsman had to straighten his sword with his foot!

What was the name of the early Roman Sword? The name of the slaves who performed at public functions is also derived from the same word.

The ideal sword needed to be hard, so that it had a sharp edge, and flexible without being brittle. The history of the swordsmith has

45

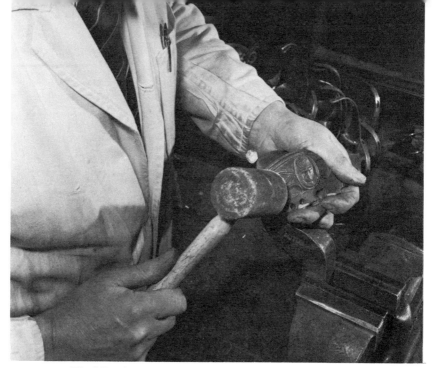

The hilt of a British naval officer's sword being finished.

centred round his attempts to tackle these two problems. To the early smith, with his poor quality materials, his lack of knowledge about metals, and his difficulty in controlling his furnace, the problems must have seemed insuperable. But eventually the swordsmiths produced a sword made of steel, hard on the outside to give a sharp edge, which was softer inside for flexibility.

The craft of the swordsmith entailed several different types of work. After the blade was made it was passed to a polisher, who worked for days to produce a mirror-like shine. Then the maker of sword furniture made the scabbard and the metal guards. The hiltmaker made the hilt and the pommel, the most intricate and elaborate part of the sword. The hilt might be plated with gold, silver or nickel, according to the customer's wishes.

Do you know which parts of the sword are the scabbard, the hilt, the pommel, the grip, the quillon, the guard?

Up until the sixteenth century the sword never really advanced

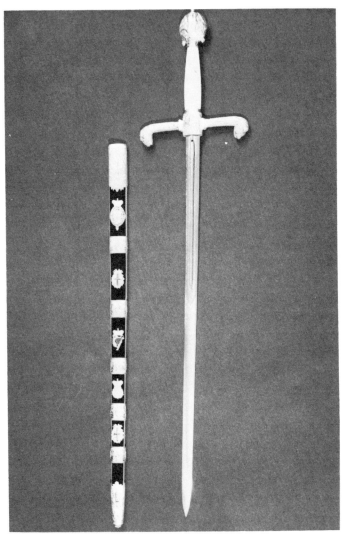

A replica of the Lord Mayor of London's Sword of State made by Wilkinson Sword Ltd in 1961. The Lord Mayor's sword is so valuable that he uses this replica on State occasions.

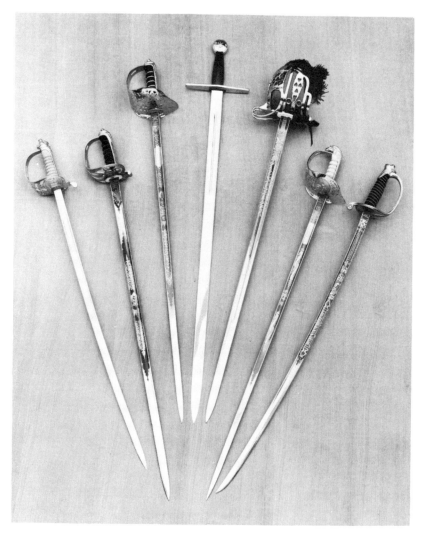

A group of modern swords. Left to right: Venezuelan military sword; Jahore police sword; replica of a thirteenth century crusader's war sword; Highland regimental officer's broadsword; Royal Air Force officer's sword; United States Marines enlisted man's sword.

beyond the straight, double-edged blade, broad at the hilt and tapering to a point. But when firearms began to be used and the use of armour died out, the science of swordsmanship made rapid advances and swords become much longer and more complicated in design. From about 1525 onwards the sword became part of the everyday civilian dress of a gentleman.

Why do you think a gentleman, walking with a lady, always walks to her right?

Duelling, with its own code of honour, became the fashionable way of settling disputes. And a man could be tried in court by combat instead of by a jury. It may surprise you to learn that trial by combat was not abolished in England until 1819. Instead of the jury deciding which man was guilty, the two men fought it out themselves, and whoever won was considered the innocent one.

Have you read any books which describe a duelling match? The Three Musketeers *by Alexandre Dumas has many exciting duels.*

A Statute of Winchester published in 1577 says that it was obligatory for every man between 15 and 40 years of age to have weapons and armour according to his means. A man with land worth £15 and goods worth 40 marks would have to have 'an hawberke, a brest plate of yron, a sworde, a knife, and an horse'. But the man with less than 20 marks in all 'shall have swordes, knives and other lesse weapons'.

Swordsmiths were never really important in England until the reign of James I (1603-1625), when skilled swordsmiths from the continent came to Britain and made it possible for England to produce sword blades which compared in quality with those from Europe. In 1620 an important smithy opened on Houslow Heath for making sword blades. This smithy supplied a large number of swords for the Civil War.

What do you know about the Civil War? When was it? What was it about?

The Wilkinson Sword Company, which was established in 1772, still produces some 15,000 swords a year, though 80 per cent of them are exported to nearly every country in the world. The swords range from standard Service types to special commemorative swords and presentation swords. They cost from a few pounds to several hundreds of pounds. Wilkinson keep forty employees busy in their factory, so you can see that the craft of the swordsmith has not completely died out.

6. Craft Guilds

Mediaeval craftsmen felt the need to band together for companionship and mutual aid and protection, rather like the Trade Unions of today, so they formed 'fraternities' or craft guilds. It may surprise you to learn that even today there are eighty-four Guilds, or Livery Companies, in the City of London. In London craftsmen of the same kind lived near to each other in a particular area of the town. For example the shoemakers gathered around Shoemaker Row, the seamstresses around Threadneedle Street and Petticoat Lane.

Perhaps you can guess, from the names of the streets, which other areas were popular with particular craftsmen?

As a result of this localising of trades the craft guilds came into being. The guilds controlled the standard of workmanship of the craftsmen, and also provided a strong religious background and community spirit.

One of the first guilds, still in existence today, is that of the

51

Weavers, whose dues to the Crown are recorded in the Exchequer Roll of 1130. Before the end of the twelfth century there were guilds for bakers, pepperers, clothworkers, butchers, turners, cooks, and coopers. Gradually the guilds became more and more powerful, and so their influence spread throughout England and generally raised the standard of workmanship. The mediaeval kings, realising what a good thing this was, granted them charters which gave special rights and powers of jurisdiction. Their laws were very strict. Special 'searchers' travelled around the country inspecting the goods and prices, and strict punishments were dealt out to anyone who failed to come up to standard.

Do you know how the Government deals with standards and prices of goods today?

The guilds had a more festive side, too. There were regular feasts and pageants, and any profits were used to help the poor. Each guild had a patron saint, and sumptuous feasts were held on the saints' days. In fact the whole municipal, industrial, and social life of the Middle Ages centred upon the guilds.

The City of London was governed by the members of the guilds, and they elected the Lord Mayor, as they still do today.

Which building is the civic centre of the City of London?

Until 1835 membership of a guild was the only way you could become a Freeman, or Citizen of the City of London, and be allowed to vote for the Lord Mayor.

Do you know who is the present Lord Mayor of London?

Today there are over twelve thousand members who are entitled to wear 'livery', or clothing, of their Companies. The word livery used to mean the allowances of food and wine which were granted to the servants, as well as clothing, in feudal times. Today, when an applicant takes his oath as a Liveryman, he is clothed with the livery—that is, the gown and hood.

Many of today's Livery Companies have been formed during the

52

Coat of Arms of the Worshipful Company of Weavers. The coats of arms of the Livery Companies come from their original trade signs. Not many of these have survived except for the barber's pole and the three balls of the pawn-broker. When a Guild wanted a device to display on a banner, or to use as a seal, it often adopted a design which contained some symbol of the calling of its members. A crest, supporters, and a motto completed the elaborate design.

last three centuries, and new ones are always coming along. Some, such as the Hatband Makers, Starch Makers, and Longbow-string Makers, have fallen by the wayside.

In 1914 a City Livery Club was founded, whose aim is to uphold and strengthen the traditions and privileges of the ancient guilds, and to encourage the Liverymen to exercise their rights as citizens of the City of London.

In the Middle Ages the most usual way of getting admission to a guild was by serving an apprenticeship. At the age of twelve a boy would be apprenticed to a master craftsman for about seven years. In return for a fee, the master would teach him the craft and feed and clothe him. At the end of the apprenticeship the boy would

Coat of Arms of the Worshipful Company of Basketmakers. The blazon (the correct description of a coat of arms) reads: 'Azure three cross baskets in pale, between a prime and an iron on the dexter and a cutting knife and an outsticker the blades downwards on the sinister also in pale argent. And for the crest, on a wreath of colours. A child in a cradle rocked at the head by a girl and at the foot by a boy both vested proper.'

submit a sample of his work to the guild. If this was of a good standard, he could pay a fee to admit himself to the Company's Livery.

The guild tradition remained important until the Industrial Revolution, when factories and commercialism took over. But to this day each guild still has its ancient rights and customs, and members look forward to their annual banquets. The Vintners and Dyers still perform their Swan Upping ceremony on the Thames to remind us that they are the only persons—other than the Queen—privileged to own these birds.

Do you know what happens at the Swan Upping ceremony? When is it?

54

The watermen of the Thames still keep up their annual race for Doggett's Coat and Badge under the supervision of the Fishmongers' Company.

Do you know who Doggett was, and why he started this race in 1716?

7. The Basketmaker

What is this man carrying on his back?

He looks rather like a beetle, doesn't he? But in fact he is carrying. his boat, called a coracle. This is a type of boat made in the same way as a basket, which was specially designed for river and coastal transport. They have been in use since Roman times, and are still made and used today in remote parts of Wales and in the Fen-lands. The farmers find they are ideal vessels to use while dipping sheep, as they are small and light, and easy to steer between the animals. Fishermen use them for fly-fishing. The coracle is made of a woven framework of willow lathes, and is propelled by a single paddle.

You may have. made baskets in handicraft lessons at school, but have you ever wondered who first made baskets and what they were used for? In fact basketmaking was one of the first crafts: people have been using baskets since 3000 BC. How do we know this? Archaeologists have found impressions of coiled baskets on pottery made at that time by the Egyptians. Coiled baskets of the

56

William Dew with his coracle.

The frame of a coracle and a finished coracle. The single paddle is used for propelling the boat.

same type are still used to this day in Egypt and Palestine, where people carry them on their heads.

American Indians used baskets for all kinds of purposes, from cradles to those containing objects needed in the next world that were put into the grave. Basketmaking was women's work, and the Indian girl made baskets for her future home, just as English girls prepare their bottom drawer.

Make a list of baskets an Indian girl might get ready for her new home.

In England the first people to make baskets were the Celts, and to this day all kinds of traditional basketwork is still being made. During the Roman occupation British exports consisted of copper and tin, lime and chalk, cattle and hides, corn and cheese, horses and dogs, pearls and slaves—with only one manufactured article—basketware.

58

The coat of arms of the Basketmakers' Company.

Basketware is no longer our chief manufactured export. Make a list of the articles that you believe are our major exports.

There still exists in the City of London a Basketmakers' Company, or Guild. This was established in 1569, four hundred years ago! The Guild's coat-of-arms has a crest of a hooded wicker cradle, and underneath the four most-used tools of the basketmaker—the prime, the cutting knife, the iron and the outsticker. In 1937 a Royal Charter was granted to the Worshipful Company of Basket-makers by King George VI, and Queen Mary, who was very interested in British handicrafts, became an Honorary Member.

Try and find out which other crafts still have a guild among the ancient fraternities of the City of London.

It was the job of the Wardens of the Guild to inspect all the basketware and to 'denounce all such as they found unlawful, not well and workmanlike and strongly made, and wrought with good and reasonable stuff'.

'Upsetting' a waste paper basket.

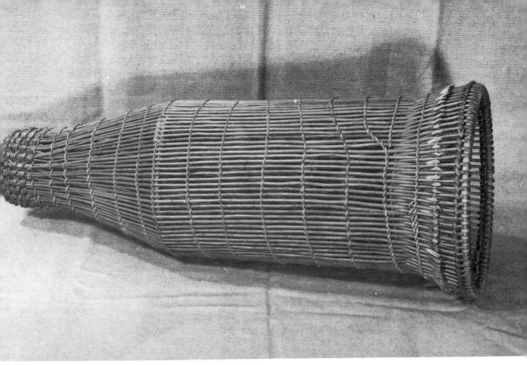

An eel grig.

Today baskets are still made in the same way as they were many hundreds of years ago. The main material has always been osier, which is a kind of willow. Beds of osier are planted specially for this purpose. Before the rods can be used, the bark must be stripped off.

You have probably danced 'Strip the Willow' at school. Now you know what the origin of this folk dance was.

The stripping was usually done by the women and children, using a tool called a brake. The prepared rods are described by the basketmaker in traditional terms: short rods are known as luke or tack; and then going up in size, short-small, long-small, three-penny, middleboro, and great. The rods are soaked in water before they are used. When they are ready, the basketmaker pegs them into a frame and weaves them firmly together into the chosen shape.

In the olden days the basketmaker did his work at home. He sat

61

Employees of Thomas Smith Ltd, making Sussex trugs.

on the ground, a lapboard between his knees, and his tools all round him on the floor.

If you make baskets at school you probably use cane. This was only introduced into England at the beginning of this century. It is much easier to work with than willow.

I expect all of you will have at least one type of basket in your home—a laundry basket, a shopping basket, a waste-paper basket—have a look and see what material it is made of.

There are several interesting baskets which you won't find in your home, and which are not much used today. Lobster pots, or baskets, for catching lobsters and crabs, are still made in the Isle of Wight. They are shaped like a bell, so that the shellfish can get in easily, but can't get out again. Eel traps were used until quite recently in the Fenlands, where they were called grigs. A type of fishbasket, called Maund, is still used in some out-of-the-way places.

The name Maundy Thursday is derived from Maund. What happens on that day?

Spelks were used for carrying coal and potatoes. And one very interesting basket—which I hope is not needed today—is the bug trap to put under pillows. These were used until very recently in France. The baskets were put under pillows at night, and in the morning they were shaken out and the insects destroyed!

About the middle of the nineteenth century a man called Thomas Smith invented a basket made of plaited rushes, which is called a Sussex trug. He exhibited it at the Great Exhibition of 1851. Queen Victoria saw it there and ordered several for her own use. They are now mainly used as gardening baskets.

What do you know about the Great Exhibition of 1851? Where was it held?

8. The Potter

Pottery is as popular today as it was thousands of years ago. The difference is that today we use it mainly for decorative purposes, and it is a luxury to own some. In prehistoric times pots were the most essential domestic equipment. Modern studio potteries flourish all over the country, particularly in tourist areas. It is one of the few crafts that has not died with the invention of modern materials and methods. In fact, because of modern mass production, people seem even more determined to keep the potter's craft alive.

What materials are used today for domestic equipment?

Modern studio potteries are not really much different from those of prehistoric times. Some potters still mould their pots by hand, and even the potter's wheel is not a new invention. The Greeks were the first people to 'throw' pots on a rotating wheel. The wheel meant that the Greek potter could produce symmetrical pots, and do so more quickly. It was many centuries before the potter's wheel reached this country.

Josiah Wedgwood's pottery shop.

Thousands of years ago man discovered that certain earths became plastic and could be moulded when they were wet. These were the earths with a high content of clay.

Do you know which areas clay comes from in this country?

Old potteries are always found near beds of local clay, because it is a difficult material to transport.

Prehistoric man also discovered that if the earth was left to dry in the sun it became hard and brittle. Further experiments produced crude, roughly shaped pots for cooking and carrying water. They were put into the middle of a hot glowing fire to make them hard. These early pots were porous and fragile, but they were the first domestic utensils that the prehistoric woman had in her home.

Some of the pots were made stronger by first weaving a willow basket and then impressing the wet clay both inside and outside.

65

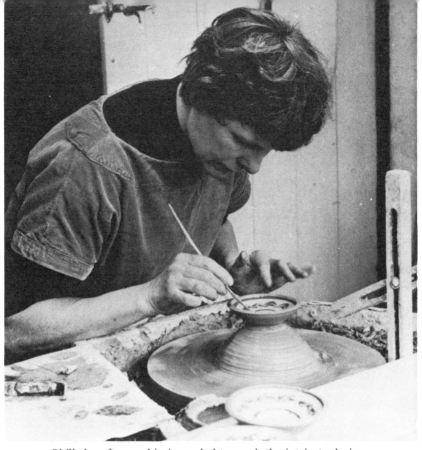

Skilled craftsmanship is needed to work the intricate designs.

You can see how important both basketwork and pottery were to those early housewives.

As well as the studio potteries which make pots by hand, there are, of course, many firms making mass-produced pottery today. Even this is not as modern as it sounds. The Romans were the first people to do repetitive production. They invented a way of making pots in moulds. During the firing in the kiln the pot shrank inside the mould so that it could be removed easily. The mould was then used over and over again.

Do you know the names of any firms that make pottery or china? Look on the bottom of your dinner plates or coffee mugs, and see if there is a name there.

A selection of goods produced by a modern studio pottery.

Craftsmen at work in the Wedgwood Factory.

If you see the name Wedgwood, you can be sure it is very good china indeed, for the firm of Josiah Wedgwood Ltd is one of the most famous of china manufacturers. Mr. Wedgwood was a characteristic figure of the late eighteenth century, when industry was beginning to move towards mass production, but had not yet lost its taste and craftsmanship. He is typical of the fine bourgeois life of eighteenth century England. At this time there was much rivalry among European and Asian countries to produce the finest china. English Chelsea, Bow, Derby and Worcester china was as fine as any. But Mr. Wedgwood catered for a larger market by making his china cheap enough for ordinary people to buy. He worked hard at new scientific methods and new designs, and even promoted turnpikes and canals in order to reduce the cost of his transport. During this time pewter went out of daily household use and was replaced with china.

Kilns at the Wedgwood Factory.

Selection of Wedgwood china produced in the middle of the eighteenth century.

Some people feel that mass produced goods cannot be the work of craftsmen. But at every china factory the hand workman is one of the most important people. Extremely skilled craftsmanship is needed to 'throw' plates and cups, and to paint on the designs.

Many schools teach pottery these days, so you may know exactly how pots are made. One of the first methods the potter learns is 'pinching'. The potter takes a small ball of clay, forces his thumb down the middle almost to the bottom, and then pinches with his hand and thumb, turning the ball round and round at the same time. The sides gradually get thinner and thinner.

Prehistoric woman almost certainly made her cooking pots like this, or by 'coiling'.

Can you explain how pots are made by the coiling method?

70

Firing pottery needs a great deal of skill because it can so easily crack if the temperature is wrong. It must have been very difficult to regulate the heat of the kiln before electricity and gas were used. Most types of pottery are fired twice, the glaze being applied after the first firing.

Do you know what the first firing is called?

In Britain the Romans made much fine pottery, but when they left only a few itinerant potters worked to supply local needs. Mediaeval pottery was nowhere near the high standards of the Greeks and Romans. The pots were clumsy, often misshapen, and covered with a glaze of green, brown or yellow. Any decoration was just scratched on, or stuck on in wadges of clay. It was during the fifteenth century that potteries were established at various centres, such as London, Staffordshire, Derbyshire and Cheshire. From then until the present day potters have been experimenting with all sorts of methods, materials and designs.

9. London Crafts, 1422

The Company of Brewers prepared a list of trades and crafts being carried out in London in 1422, to be kept with their documents and records. 'A list of names of all the crafts exercised in London from of old, and still continuing in this ninth year of King Henry V and here set down in case it may in any wise profit the hall and Company of Brewers.'

As you read the list, see if you know exactly what each craftsman did. How many of them still exist today? What new crafts are there today which are not on this list?

Mercers, Grocers, Drapers, Fishmongers, Goldsmiths, Vintners, Skinners, Tailors, Saddlers, Ironmongers, Girdlers, Cordwainers, Haberdashers, Cutlers, Armourers, Weavers, Fullers, Dyers, Plasterers, Carpenters, Pewterers, Plumbers, Joiners, Founders, Leathersellers, Bakers, Shearmen, Lorimers (makers of horse furniture), Waxchandlers, Tallowchandlers, Tanners, Curriers, Pouchmakers, Bowyers, Fletchers, Horners, Spurriers (makers of spurs), Hatters, Cofferers, Pointmakers, Wiremakers, Cardmakers (makers of

combs for carding wool), Pinners, Whittawyers, Leather-
dyers, Stainers, Hostillers, Cooks, Piemakers, Bellmakers,
Corsours (horse dealers), Chariotmakers, Broochmakers,
Jewellers, Paternosters (makers of rosaries), Turners, Book-
binders, Writers of Texts, Stationers, Poulterers, Clockmakers,
Chapemakers (makers of metal plates for the points of scab-
bards), Sheders (combers), Malemakers (trunk makers),
Tablemakers, Lockyers, Fourbours (polishers), Burlesters
(cloth dressers), Lateners (workers in brass), Potters, Stuffers,
Fruiterers, Cheesemongers, Stringers, Basketmakers, Barbers,
Brewers, Butchers, Tapicers (tapestry makers), Broderers,
Painters, Salters, Brasiers (brass workers), Smiths, Hurers
(hatters), Woodmongers, Writers of Courtletters, Limners
(artists), Leches (doctor), Ferrours (ironworkers), Copper-
smiths, Upholders (upholsterers), Galochemakers, Carvers,
Glassiers, Felmongers (dealers in skins), Woolmen, Corn-
mongers, Blacksmiths, Ropers, Lanternmakers, Haymongers,
Bottlemakers, Marblers, Netmakers, Potmakers, Glovers,
Hosiers, Orglemakers (organ makers), Soapmakers.

This is a very impressive list isn't it? During the fifteenth century
the government of London trade was conducted by the members
of the large merchant companies, rather than by the democracy of
manufacturing guilds which were so important in Chaucer's time.
The Mercers, Grocers, Drapers, Fishmongers and Goldsmiths
supplied nearly all the mayors and aldermen, and their businesses
included exports from overseas, on which they made a great deal
of profit. The merchants had their own ships, houses and agents,
and this aristocracy ruled the capital wisely. They took no part in
the wars which were going on in other parts of the country.

Which wars were these? What were they about?

In 1422 a famous man was born. He started a trade in England in
1477 which was a very important step towards progress.

Do you know who he was?

10. The Thatcher

What material is the roof of the house you live in made of?

This will probably depend on the area you live in, for more often, than not, particularly with old houses, the roofs are made of local material. Perhaps you are very lucky and live in a picturesque cottage with a thatched roof? In any case you will have seen thatched roofs on country houses. But it might surprise you to learn that there are over 800 thatchers working full time today maintaining and renewing those thatched roofs.

The craft of thatching has been practised in Britain since before the Norman Conquest. It was the earliest way of building roofs. In those days the materials used were much more varied: reeds, rushes, broom, heather, even bracken. Then the thatchers began to use cultivated barley, wheat and rye straw. Today the two materials used are wheat straw—called long straw—and reed: Norfolk reed or combed wheat reed. Reed tends to be more popular because the introduction of the combine harvester, which trusses all

74

The house in these two pictures used to have a long-straw roof; a few years
ago it was re-thatched in combed wheat reed. The pictures show very clearly
how different the two methods look. The long straw roof in the top picture
has a smoother, more plastic appearance, whereas the combed wheat reed
below has a stiff, close-cropped, brush-like texture.

Working on a long-straw roof, raking down the course.

the straw into bundles, meant that there was no longer any straw suitable for thatching.

Next time you see a thatched building, see if you can tell which method has been used.

Thatching has not changed much since the Middle Ages. The manors in the fourteenth century kept accounts of their tools and equipment, and some of these mention leggetts, ledgers, spars, and brotches, all of which are used by the thatcher today.

The first step in thatching a long straw roof is 'spar-making'. This means getting hazel or willow rods ready for using as pegs, and for binding the thatch to keep it together. The next job is to get the straw laid out on the ground ready to use. It is always wetted before it is used to make it more flexible. Then the straw is made into 'yelms'—bundles of straw eighteen inches wide and five inches thick. These yelms are fixed to the roof slanting upwards from the eaves to the ridge until the whole roof is covered. They are held fast by tarred twine, which is threaded through an enormous thatching needle.

In the old days, when craftsmen were not very businesslike, a thatcher would just look at a roof and give a verbal estimate of the cost of thatching it. Today the thatcher draws up a detailed estimate of all his costs and submits an estimate in writing. An average sized roof might cost about £400 to thatch.

Suggest what items of expenditure the thatcher would take into account when drawing up his estimate.

When a roof is thatched with combed wheat reed, the reed is made into bundles and tied with string before attaching them to the roof, where they are laced together to keep them firm. A tool called a leggett—a sort of board with grooves— is used to dress the bundles neatly into line. A bundle of wheat reed is called a 'nitch' and should weigh twenty-eight pounds. Combed wheat reed is sometimes called 'Devon weed', because this method of thatching is very popular in Devon.

Working on a combed wheat reed roof. The two helpers on the ladders are each carrying a 'nitch' of wheat reed.

A roof thatched with long straw will probably last about fifty years if it is sheltered from the wind. Norfolk reed thatching will last up to a hundred years as it is a more durable material. If you live in a house with a thatched roof you will know that it is very practical as well as pretty. A thatched roof keeps a house cool in summer and warm in winter.

Can you suggest some methods we might use to make our homes warmer in winter by insulating against the cold?

Working on a Norfolk reed roof. The thatcher is driving hooks into the reed with a claw hammer. These hold the reed firm.

One of the disadvantages of thatched roofs is that there is a greater risk of fire. Today it is possible to soak the thatching material in a special liquid which makes it less inflammable. In the old days large iron hooks used to be hung in prominent places in the village, so that, if a fire broke out, the burning thatch could be quickly pulled down before it fell in and set light to the house.

Along the ridge of the roof the thatch was pulled over from each side and firmly woven together to stop the rain getting in. Sometimes the thatcher decorated the ridge, or cut it straight across.

When you are looking at a thatched roof, look at the ridge and see how the thatcher has finished it off.

11. Women's Crafts

Perhaps your mother goes out to work to make money for all those little extras you wouldn't have on your father's wages? In days gone by women *had* to work to help support the family, because the working man's wages were never enough. Your mother might work in a shop or a factory, but in the earlier days there were no such places for a woman to work, and anyway there were no nurseries where she could leave her young children. So in the intervals between doing the housework and looking after the children, many mothers practised a 'cottage' craft at home. Often a women would earn as much as her husband did in his full-time job.

Lace-making was very popular in the seventeenth and eighteenth centuries, as lace was very much in fashion for both women's and men's clothing. Up until the seventeenth century, from the reign of Queen Elizabeth I, stiff ruffs edged with lace had been popular. Then soft falling collars of heavy, rich lace became the fashion.

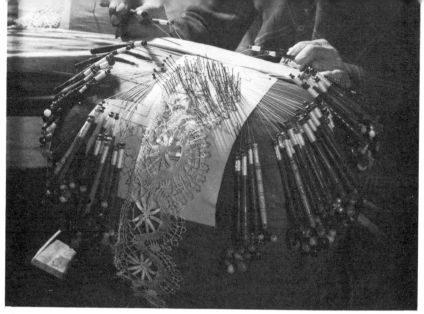

A woman making pillow lace. Notice the bobbins hanging down on both sides of the pillow.

Next time you visit an art gallery, pay particular attention to portraits. Are they wearing lace? If so which kind?

Lace was very expensive because there were never enough women to make it. This meant that people began to smuggle lace from abroad. The excise duties were very heavy. Smugglers hid the lace in all sorts of places, even in coffins containing real corpses!

On which items from abroad does one have to pay excise duties today?

Lace became so popular that in some districts lace schools were set up where children were taught the craft so that they could help their mothers.

There were two kinds of lace: needlepoint and pillow lace. Needlepoint lace was worked with a needle and thread. Pillow lace, sometimes called bobbin lace, was done by plaiting and weaving threads wound on to bobbins. The lace was made on a firm pillow.

The stand on which the pillow rested while the lace-maker worked. On the right is a lace-maker's light.

Making bobbins was another craft in itself. A bobbin was a small, shaped piece of wood, bone or ivory. Often they were elaborately carved and adorned with mottoes.

The lace-maker did most of her work sitting at her cottage door, with the lace-pillow on a stand before her. But in winter and at night it was necessary to have artificial light. A special lace-maker's light was used. This was a glass globe which stood on a table with a lighted candle placed near it in such a way that the rays were reflected by the glass directly on to the work.

Not many women make lace today. Fashions change, and by the end of the nineteenth century no one wanted to wear lace. It is still sometimes used for wedding dresses and christening robes. All the royal babies are christened in a gown of Honiton lace.

Women who didn't make lace would often be quilters. When you hear the word 'quilt' don't think of the bulky, terylene filled bedcover you probably use at home. These quilts were made of two layers of cotton, linen or silk, lined with scoured sheep's wool. The quilts were beautifully embroidered with designs of flowers, leaves, shells, spirals, waves and crowns.

A quilt took a long time to make but it was a thing of real beauty and lasted for years.

Quilting was not only for putting on beds, but was also fashionable for clothing, for both men and women. In the eighteenth century textile printing was developed and quilting lost its popularity.

What do you think might have caused the decline in the use of quilts as bedcovers?

Quilts are still made in some places, particularly in Durham, Wales and Northern Ireland, but they are so expensive to make that they are real luxuries today.

A quilt was made on a frame which held the two pieces of material evenly together. A bed-spread would be on a frame about eight feet tall, so that as many as six women could work on it at once. Such gatherings became known as 'quilting parties'.

Quilting is an old craft, probably first done in this country in the fourteenth century. In mediaeval inventories quilts are often mentioned. For example one historian has written that 'in May 1540 Katherine Howard, afterwards wife of Henry VIII, received 23 quilts of quilted sarsenet out of the Royal Wardrobe, as a sign of Royal favour.'

When did Katherine Howard become Henry VIII's queen? Who were his other queens?

Another interesting craft, though it was not usually done as a money-making occupation, was the making of corn dollies. You

When the design of the quilt has been decided, templates of the various motives were made of stiff cardboard. The template was placed on top of the material and the quilter scratched round the outline with a needle. When the template was removed, the scratched line would show clearly enough to be sewn through. A more modern method is to rub chalk round the edges of the template.

Quilts were made on a frame which held the two pieces of material evenly together.

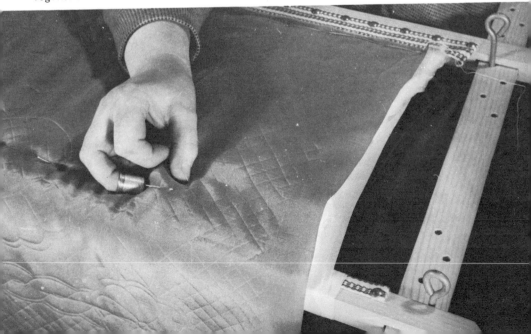

A finished quilt.

might think a corn 'dolly' is like a child's doll, but in fact it is a sort of idol made of straw, and doesn't necessarily look like a doll at all. It might be a cross, a bell, a horn, a spray, a horseshoe, or keys. Different parts of the country had different symbols.

Primitive people, when they began to till the soil to provide food, worshipped the Goddess of Fertility, the Corn Mother. The women did the farm-work in those days, and they made straw images in honour of the Corn Mother so that she would bring them luck and fertility. This custom has survived throughout the ages, and in England has become part of our Harvest Festivals, though the dollies are no longer idols, as in pagan times, but part of the decoration. Both after sowing the seed and reaping the harvest, corn dollies were carried in procession round the fields:

86

Corn dollies like these have been made for hundreds of years. In this picture are, left to right, a Mordiford from Herefordshire; a Corn Maiden; a Barton Turf from Norfolk.

A Norfolk lantern—a more elaborate corn dolly about eighteen inches long.

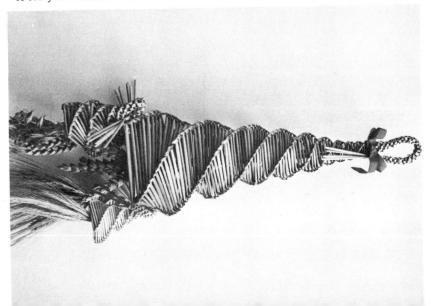

the first time to make the seeds grow, the second in celebration.

In the ceremony of the last sheaf the life force of the field was preserved in the corn dolly, made from the corn of the last sheaf. The Corn Mother was supposed to live in the cornfield and she died when the corn was cut. The corn dolly was carried to the farmhouse to be kept until the following year to ensure the continuance of the crops.

In these days of modern machinery and methods farmers are not so dependent on the weather for a good harvest, so the rituals are no longer observed. But some craftswomen still make corn dollies for decorations and for harvest festivals.

You might like to try making corn dollies yourself. There are two books you can read: The Golden Dolly *by M. Lambeth and* Decorative Straw Work *by L. Sandford and P. Davis.*

12. Surnames

Have you ever wondered where your surname comes from? Surnames are the most personal things we possess, yet we nearly always take them for granted. Your surname is your heritage, passed down through the centuries, a legacy from the past.

Most surnames fall into one of four groups: local surnames, surnames of relationship, nicknames, and surnames of trade or occupation. Occupational surnames originated from the mediaeval practice of quoting a man's trade, followed by his first name, such as Baker John. Many of these trades may have vanished centuries ago, but they still live on in our surnames. Some have remained almost unaltered, but others, distorted and changed through the years, bear little resemblence to their original spelling or pronunciation.

Names of occupation amount to about 16 per cent of English surnames. The most familiar name of all, *Smith*, comes into this group. If *Smith* is your name you can feel justifiably proud, for smiths were very important members of the community. The reason why there are so many *Smiths* today is that there was one in every village or hamlet. It is one of the few names recorded before the Norman invasion. There are many derivations of this name: if you are called *Arrowsmith*, *Arsmith* or *Harismith*, your ancestors were smiths who made arrow heads.

The comparative numbers in which a name survives are very significant. The most popular names today are those of tradesmen who were particularly numerous or important in mediaeval times. If you look in any telephone directory you will find a long list of *Clarks* and *Taylors*.

The clerk, like the smith, was an important person because he had a skill that was much in demand—he could read and write. A tailor in those days made shoes and hats as well as clothes, so there are plenty of *Taylors* today, but not many *Shoemakers* or *Hatters*. The cordwainers made expensive, fashionable shoes, so there were not many of them, and not many people with the surname *Cordwainer* today.

Miller and *Baker* are common names, and this is not surprising since they provided the most important food. You might expect *Plowman* to be common too, since the ploughman toiled to grow the wheat. But manual labour was not considered important, it was the smith who forged the plowshare and the baker who made the bread who mattered.

If your forebearers were in the Wool Trade you might be called *Weaver*, *Webb*—a very old name for a weaver, or *Webster*; *Spinner* or *Spinster*; *Walker*, *Fuller*, *Tucker*, or *Lister*. And if they were woodcraftsmen you might be *Turner* or *Cooper (Cowper)*.

Transport was important, and most manors had carts, driven by *Carters*. Carts were sometimes called wains or waynes, so we get *Wainer*, *Wainman*, *Wenman* or *Weyman*. The men who built the carts were *Cartwrights*, *Wainwrights*, and *Wheelers*.

Other familiar names from rural life are *Fisher*, *Fowler*, *Shepherd*, *Farmer* and *Hogarth* (pig or hog farmer).

From the commercial trades we get *Merchant* and *Marchant*. Also *Chapman*—the English word for one who bought and sold, gradually superseded by the French 'marchand'.

SURNAMES

London has always been a city of specialist trades and crafts, so whereas in the country the smith dealt with all kinds of metal work, in London it was divided among many crafts. Locksmiths gave us the names *Locker* and *Lockyer*; knife-smiths gave us *Cutler*; nail-smiths *Naylor* and so on.

See if you can find out where your surname comes from. You will find books in your local library to help you.

How many of your friends and neighbours have names which come from trades and crafts?

13. The Coachbuilder

From the Highway Code of 1816:

> In congested traffic, never overtake on the right.
> Beware of omnibus and fiacre drivers.
> If there are children around, slow down and take great care.

The Highway Code hasn't altered much since 1816, so it is strange, isn't it, to think that it once applied to horse-drawn coaches and carriages? Traffic jams are not a phenomenon of the 1970s: in the nineteenth century London's streets were thronged with Landaus, Victorias, Hansom Cabs and Hackney Coaches. Charles Dickens described a Hackney Coach in *Sketches by Boz*, in 1835:

> 'There is a hackney-coach stand under the very window at which we are writing; there is only one coach on it now, but it is a fair specimen of the class of vehicles to which we have alluded—a great, lumbering, square concern of dingy yellow colour (like a bilious brunette), with very small glasses, but very large frames; the panels are ornamented with a faded coat of arms, in shape something like a dissected bat, the axletree is red, and the majority of the wheels are green.'

The London to Dorking stage coach, 1880.

Many of Dickens' novels describe the transport of the nine-teenth century. Can you think of other examples?

The first English coach was built by Walter Rippon in 1555. They became popular about nine years later when Queen Elizabeth I appointed a Dutchman, William Boonen, to be her coachman. Coaches at that time were completely open, but in the early seventeenth century they made them with coach-boxes on the bodies.

The first stage coaches and mail coaches appeared at this time too. The stage coach carried six passengers inside, and the poorer people were allowed to cling to the luggage on the roof. You can imagine what an uncomfortable journey they had: the coaches were always overturning on the rough roads, and being held up at pistol point by highwaymen. The red-coated guard with his blunderbuss was kept very busy protecting the unfortunate travellers.

Coaches were soon travelling regularly from London to all the large towns. In 1754 the 'Flying Coach' took four and a half days

A dog cart.

to get from London to Manchester.

How long would it take to make this journey today?

The Royal Mail coach drove at the shattering speed of eight miles an hour.

In the second half of the eighteenth century turnpikes were erected along the main highways. Coach drivers had to pay a toll which went towards the cost of repairing and maintaining the roads.

Do you know which two men were responsible for the improvement of roads?

With better roads, travel and communication were improved. Many country people travelled to London for the first time. Arthur Young, a chronicler of the time, observed in his *Farmer's Letters* in 1771, that young men and women were leaving their country villages to come to London, which hadn't been easy be-

A Clarence.

fore when the stage coach was so slow and expensive: 'A country fellow, one hundred miles from London, jumps on a coach box in the morning, and for eight or ten shillings gets to town by night.'

There were many more coaches and carriages on the roads now. Better roads meant that private carriages could be lighter and more elegant. To drive a lady in a phaeton built for two, with its high wheels and a smart pair of horses, was a fashionable pastime. The 'Golden Age' of coaching had begun!

Coachbuilding needed many different craftsmen for all the different types of work involved. The body-makers made the wooden body-work; the carriage-makers built the undercarriage; the blacksmiths made all the decorative ironwork, such as steps, doorhandles, lamp brackets, and hood frames. Then there were the wheelwrights who made the wheels; the curriers who provided all the leather upholstery and fittings; the trimmers who supplied lace edgings, tasselled cords, and blinds. Most important of all, of course, were the designers and painters. Coach painting required a

One of the first petrol-driven, four wheeled British cars, built in 1895.

great deal of skill, as most coaches were painted in the family colours, with large heraldic crests.

The coachbuilders worked hard for twelve hours a day, six days a week. Their average weekly wage was £2.00-£3.00.

How does this compare with the working week of a car factory worker today?

One of the best known coachbuilding firms was Thrupp and Maberley, started by Mr. Joseph Thrupp in 1760, when George III had just become king. Thrupp's design and craftsmanship were so good that his coaches were easily recognisable on the street. Competition between coachbuilders was keen, and there were annual prizes for those with the best designs.

THE COACHBUILDER

Each firm tried to design their own distinctive carriage, so there were numerous different types on the roads. Some were driven by liveried coachmen: the Town Coach was one of the first of these. The Town Coach was a large vehicle drawn by four horses, and seating four passengers. At first they were used by the nobility, but later they became taxis and were put on the streets for hire, and called Hackney Coaches.

With the coming of the railway in the early nineteenth century long-distance travel by coach became obsolete.

Do you know who designed the first locomotive? Where was the first railway line laid?

Carriages were used only for local travelling, but with the invention of the motor car they too became out-of-date. English coachbuilders either went out of business altogether or started making motor car bodies. Thrupp and Maberley built a very interesting vehicle for the Queen of Spain. Called an Electric Victoria, it ran on a battery which weighed two hundred-weight, and could be driven at 10 miles per hour for up to sixty miles.

The Daimler Motor Co. Ltd was launched in 1896, and exhibited several petrol-driven cars at London's first ever motor show. The Prince of Wales rode in one of the new vehicles, which helped to reassure the public that they were safe.

Who was the Prince of Wales at that time?

What is now the Rolls-Royce Company was started by a coachbuilder called Mulliner in 1897.

Do you know the correct name of the Flying Lady mascot on the bonnet of these world-famous cars?

Do you know who designed it and when it was first used?

If you live in London or happen to be visiting it in November you will be able to see the Lord Mayor of London's famous Golden

Coach. This coach, carved and gilded, with painted panels on the side by Cipriani, is so heavy that it has to be drawn by six horses. The Lord Mayor's procession, first recorded in 1215, was intended to give the people a chance of seeing their new Lord Mayor as he drove to his sovereign to swear allegiance. Today he takes the oath at the Law Courts.

Can you find out when the coach was built and how much it weighs?

Today there are hardly any coachbuilders left, and most of the coaches are in museums. Fortunately in England we can still see the Queen in her coach when she drives to State functions.

If you want to see more beautiful coaches, you can visit the Royal Mews at Buckingham Palace, where you will see the Gold State Coach, the Glass State Coach, and many others.

14. Fairs and Markets

Autumn was the season for fairs. The farmer's year was complete, the harvest gathered in, and it was time for a little merry-making before the winter set in. It was also time to hire employees for the coming year.

Many of the autumn fairs were Hiring, or Mop Fairs. Everyone who was looking for a new job stood in a long row, with some mark of their occupation on them so that prospective employers could see what their job was. Shepherds wore a tuft of wool in their hats, or carried a crook; carters carried a whip; maids carried a mop or wore a white apron. Engagements were made by the year, and when a bargain was struck, the worker received a 'fasten-penny' or earnest money, with which he bought a ribbon to replace the token of his trade.

A few weeks after the Mop Fair a Runaway Mop Fair was held in the same place. This gave a second chance to those still without work, and to those who hadn't settled down in their new jobs.

A mediaeval fair.

This seems rather a precarious way of getting a job, doesn't it? How would you set about getting a job today?

Hiring Fairs were common all through the nineteenth century, but were abandoned at the beginning of this one.

Fairs and markets were a great feature of mediaeval life. They were important as places to buy and sell goods, and provided a brief respite from the grimness of everyday life. Tradesmen had to pay a tax either to the king or to the landowner as rent for their stall, or for permission to stand and sell their goods in the market. The taxes and dues payable to the king were all accounted at the Court of Exchequer—so-called after the great chequered table at which all accounts were calculated with squares and counters.

100

An eighteenth century fair. Fairs provided entertainment as well as an opportunity to do business.

What is the function of The Exchequer today?

Many fairs applied to be chartered, and were then confirmed by law. Often charters were granted as a reward for services to the king. Individuals or noble families made vast revenues from the rents.

Markets were held weekly, mainly for local produce and articles of everyday use. Once or twice a year fairs were held to which merchants from overseas brought silk, spices, jewels, and linens. There were strict rules governing the markets. A hut called a 'Tolbooth' was used to accommodate the Court of Pie Powder—a special court to deal with offenders on the spot. Many tradesmen were itinerant, and it was necessary to punish them before they moved on—literally, before the dust of the fair was off their feet. The name is a corruption of the old French for pedlar—*pieds poudreux*—dusty-footed. The craft guilds organised the courts, in return for special privileges.

An old English word for buying is 'cheaping'. The merchant was a cheapman, or chapman. One street where stalls were set up in London is still known as Cheapside, and another as Eastcheap. Any towns with the prefix 'Chipping' used to be market towns.

How many can you think of?

In the twelfth and thirteenth centuries markets were often held in churchyards, and scenes of disorder and rowdiness took place round many churches and cathedrals on the feast of the patron saint. But at the time of the Reformation this was forbidden, and fairs became secular.

Perhaps most interesting of all were the Frost Fairs. There have been several occasions when the ice on the Thames was so thick that a fair could be held on it. Normal life came to a halt while Londoners enjoyed sledging, skating, eating and drinking, and watching all the usual novelties of the fair—juggling, puppets, side-shows—all on ice. Booths and shops were erected by the trades-men, and in 1684 printing presses were set up. Queen Elizabeth I enjoyed a Frost Fair in 1554, and an ox was roasted on the ice in her honour. Again in 1715 and 1739 the river froze thick enough for a fair, and the last one took place in 1814.

One of the nastiest fairs was Bartholomew Fair, which was held at Smithfield in London from 1133 to 1855. It began as a cloth fair, but soon became a gathering place for beggars, greedy friars, pedlars, public hangings and quarterings, and all kinds of grotesque entertainments. A man who lived in 1685 described it like this:

> 'Here you see the rope-dancers gett their living meerly by hazarding of their lives, and why men will pay money and take pleasure to see such dangers, is of separate and philosophical consideration. You have others who are acting fools, drunkards, and madmen, but for the same wages which they might get by honest labour, and live with credit besides. Others, if born in any monstrous shape, or have children that are such, here they celebrate their misery, and by getting of money forget how odious they are.'

Mayfair, in London, takes its name from the May Fair which

102

A late nineteenth century hiring fair. The labourers for hire are standing in a long row on the left hand side.

was granted a charter in 1689. William Hone described the entertainments of the fair in his *Everyday Book:*

> 'In the areas encompassing the market building were booths for jugglers, prize-fighters, both at cudgels and back-sword, boxing-matches, and wild beasts. The sports not under cover were mountebanks, fire-eaters, ass-racing, sausage-tables, dice-tables, up-and-downs, merry-go-rounds, bull-baiting, grinning for a hat, running for a shift, hasty-pudding eaters, eel-divers, and an infinite variety of other similar pastimes.'

15. Woodcraftsmen

Do you know what a chair-bodger is?

This odd name is that of the craftsman who made all the legs, spars and stretchers for Windsor chairs. The chair-bodger was what we call an 'itinerant craftsman' because he moved his hut from one place to another looking for fresh wood. He lived mostly in the Chilterns, as this is where the best beech woods are. Even today, when Windsor chairs are made in factories, the industry is centred around High Wycombe.

The chair-bodger's tools are simple, and this made it easy for him to move around. He would have a 'horse' for shaping the wood into spars, and then a pole lathe for shaping the chair legs. The lathe was made from flexible poles tied with string to a treadle on the ground. The wood was fixed to an iron spike and made to turn against a cutting tool by the pressure of the treadle and the spring of the pole.

Most woodcraftsmen were itinerant. The wood turner used a

A chair-bodger's hut in the Chilterns, showing the pole lathe.

similar lathe as he moved around the woods making platters, bowls, ladles and spoons. Eventually some of the wood turners started using a wheel lathe, because the old-fashioned pole lathe was very tiring. The turner used to work from six in the morning until nine at night, standing most of the time on one leg while the other operated the treadle.

Windsor chairs used at one time to be cottage furniture. There is a story that George I, caught in a thunderstorm, saw chairs like these in a cottage near Windsor and ordered some for the Castle. So they became popular elsewhere, particularly in gardens and public rooms.

There are very few woodcraftsmen left today. Modern materials and machines have forced them to give up work.

What materials can you think of that have replaced wood?

Clog-making used to be a flourishing rural industry, as in the Middle Ages clogs were worn by everyone from dairy maids to

The chair-bodger shaping chair legs on a 'horse'.

miners. Clogs were very practical as footwear. The thick wooden soles kept the wearer's feet dry on wet factory floors and muddy roads.

Today we have another, very practical, piece of footwear, named after a famous nineteenth century Duke. Do you know what it is?

Since prehistoric times craftsmen have made wattle hurdles. In the twelfth century there was a great demand for wattle hurdles on the sheep farms of Southern England. Hazel coppices were planted to provide the material.

What does the sheep farmer use today to keep his flock in check?

Today wattle hurdles are still popular as garden fencing, so there

106

A Windsor chair.

A wattle-hurdle weaver at work.

are still a few wattle hurdle weavers at work.

Before the invention of coke ovens in the eighteenth century, charcoal was much in demand as a fuel, and charcoal burning was a popular woodland craft. The charcoal burner was a very picturesque figure. He and his family lived in a primitive hut made of logs and turves beside a slow burning kiln which produced the charcoal.

What fuels do we use for heating today?

The cooper, or barrel-maker, was one of the most highly skilled of the woodcraftsmen. In the Middle Ages barrels were the standard package for butter, apples, soap and many other goods, as well as for beer and wine. The cooper had to work a seven-year apprenticeship before he became really skilled. When he was fully trained, he might work on his own as an 'itinerant' cooper, or take up employment with a brewery. His wages were low, despite his skill. During the reign of James I, a cooper might make 6d (2½p) a

The cooper—the tool he is using is called an adze.

The wheelwright's shop. The craftsman on the left is shaping a spoke for a wheel. The one on the right is using a tool called a 'spoke dog' to fit a felloe onto two spokes. The outside rim of a wheel was usually made up of six felloes.

day, plus his board and lodging. Today there are hardly any coopers left, as barrels are made of metal by machines.

The wheelwright, too, was an essential part of the village community when horses were still used for transport. Constructing a wheel was a highly skilled craft, for the whole work depended on the tightness of the joints to hold the wheel together—not on glue! A wheelwright's shop was responsible for making the whole vehicle, but the setting of the wheels so that the cart ran properly was certainly the most difficult part.

Do you know what a besom is?

I expect you have seen them being used for sweeping up leaves. It is an old-fashioned broom made of birch twigs bound together

The broom squire's yard. On the left are bundles of hazel, ash or lime stakes used for handles. On the right is a huge pile of birch twigs. These are left to mature and season for several months before they are used. In the centre are some finished besoms.

with wire. Besoms have been used since Saxon times, and were used for sweeping up the dust at home before the invention of vacuum cleaners. They are still made today in the village of Tadley, on the Hampshire-Berkshire border. A workshop there has been in existence since the sixteenth century. The besom maker was often called a 'broom squire'.

This chapter has mentioned just a few of the old woodcraftsmen. I expect you can think of several more.

111

16. Folklore and Tradition

A miner going to work the first shift would turn round and go straight home again if he met a woman on the way. A squinting woman would have been an even worse omen, as would a man with a wooden leg. A miner would never go back into his house to get something he had forgotten, but would stand at the door until it was brought to him. It was unlucky to change shifts with another miner in midweek, and for luck a cat was put into the oven or the coal tongs were hung over the mantlepiece. Miners believed that the Seven Whistlers, a group of sinister birds, cried as a warning of danger. The ghosts of dead workmates or of children were also warnings of disaster.

This probably sounds like old-fashioned nonsense to you. But have you never avoided walking under a ladder, or thought yourself lucky if a black cat ran across your path?

What other everyday superstitions can you think of?

Our ancestors, who were not as well educated or knowledgeable as we are now, had a whole folklore of beliefs and customs connected with their work, which they passed on from generation to generation. You will be surprised how many of them still exist, and how new customs and superstitions are coming into existence every day. Some of these will survive to become the folklore of the next century.

Many of the old customs may seem odd today, but to those who believed in them there was nothing strange about them at all. And if you think about it, there is usually some reason behind what may seem a ridiculous tradition. Often a tradition marked the change of season, or of life—birth, coming of age, marriage and death. Many were a sort of protection for a newly started job or a blessing on a new enterprise.

Tradition dictated that when a new ship's masts were stepped, a gold coin was placed under each of them. This custom goes back to Roman times. In England a sovereign has always been used, but the masts of the *Sir Winston Churchill* were stepped onto Churchill crowns. Four days later the masts snapped off in a high wind. Can you wonder that people follow the old customs, just in case?

It is traditional these days to launch a new ship by breaking a bottle of champagne over the bows. It used to be a custom of millers to kill a cockerel on St Martin's Eve—10th November—and sprinkle the blood onto the machinery in the mill. This was known as 'blooding the mill'. Probably champagne has just taken the place of blood.

The blacksmith has always been associated with strange beliefs. Many people believed that the smith had magical medicinal powers, and as a result he was held in awe by the rest of the community. One of the strangest customs was the 'survival test' for sick babies. The baby was laid on the anvil and seven smiths stood around it with heavy hammers and made as if to strike heated iron. If the baby was frightened, it would live, if not, then it would die. Many smiths had the reputation of being blood charmers, and the water in which they cooled the iron was said to have medicinal qualities.

113

The cooper's apprentice being rolled around the workshop in a barrel.

His initiation over, the apprentice receives his certificate.

Which good luck charm is associated with the blacksmith?

Another tradesman is supposed to bring luck, particularly at weddings. Do you know which one?

The building trade has many strange rituals. These days foundation stones of new buildings are laid with a great deal of ceremony. In the Middle Ages some kind of sacrifice was required to ensure new buildings against evil influences, so a live cat or dog would be sealed under the floorboards or behind a wall. Sometimes the sacrifice took the form of animal blood, which was used to mix the cement.

Many trades had initiation ceremonies for a young apprentice, either on his first day at work or when he had completed his apprenticeship. Some of these were mere practical jokes, others were really cruel. The most usual was for the new boy to be sent on a fool's errand. Boys were often sent for jars of elbow grease, or bubbles for a spirit level!

115

A newly qualified cooper had to go through a horrible ordeal when his apprenticeship was finished. This ceremony was called 'trussing the cooper'. The young man stood in a smoking barrel, and was plastered with soot, treacle, feather, shavings and beer. He was rolled round the workshop inside the barrel, and then taken out and tossed into the air three times.

The printers had a similar custom called 'banging out'. The apprentice was smeared with printers' ink and led in procession through all the departments of the firm.

17. The Miller and the Millwright

How much bread do you eat every week?

Bread, biscuits, cakes, pastries, pies, puddings . . . I expect you can think of a lot of things you eat that are made with flour. British flour-millers today mill 5,000,000 tons of wheat a year into flour to feed us.

But do you realise that bread made from wheat has been a large part of man's diet for thousands of years? A stone used for milling has been found that is thought to be 7500 years old.

When primitive man learned to farm cereals he began to dwell in communities, rather than to live a wandering life hunting and herding cattle. He had found a food which would keep through the winter months and which could be grown again in the summer.

Ancient civilisations used to make bread by pounding the grains of wild grasses to a coarse flour and mixing this with water to a dough. The Romans were the first people to mill grain and produce a variety of flours. They used a quern, which was two stones on top of one another, turned by a stick fitted to the upper one.

117

A quern.

The earliest type of windmill was called a post mill. It consisted of a box-like timber body which carried the sails and contained the machinery, and which was mounted on an upright 'post' on which it could be turned so that the sails faced into the wind. This, Bourn Mill in Cambridgeshire, is the older type of post mill.

The old post mills had to be turned into the wind by hand. They had a tail pole—a long piece of wood reaching from high up on the back of the mill, down to the ground, which the miller had to push round.

Grain was fed into the hole in the centre of the upper stone, and the two stones crushed the grain as one turned on top of the other. The Romans' baking was also of a very high standard, and many of today's varieties of bread were known centuries ago. For example, it is thought that the cottage loaf was first baked in Roman times.

How many different types of loaf can you think of? Do you know how much each costs?

120

This scale model of a post mill, Sprowston Mill in Norwich, shows what the inside and the machinery looked like. At the very top of the mill you can see the grain bins, which feed the grain between the two pairs of stones into the meal bins on the bottom floor of the mill. If you would like to see this model, it, and others like it, is on display in the Science Museum, London.

In this country poor people have always relied on bread for their daily existence—it formed a much larger proportion of their diet than it does of yours today.

So understandably bread has always been a subject of political significance. In the early nineteenth century people got very worried about the invention of new machinery, which they feared would put them out of work. Many of them were already suffering from hunger because the Corn Laws of 1815, which forbade the import of cheap, foreign corn, had made the price of bread rise so high they could not afford it.

Which Prime Minister repealed the Corn Laws in 1845, and had to resign because the wealthy farmers were so angry?

The workers began to smash machines and burn down new factories.

There was a special name for these rioters, what was it?

New mills were being built that could grind 200 sacks of wheat in a day, using only twelve men. Before that each mill would grind one sack a day, using 2 men. So there were 400 men and 200 mills being used to do what 12 men and 1 mill could do.

William Cobbett was a man who understood the working people, and he wanted to try and stop the trouble that he saw coming. He wanted to show the people that progress and reform were inevitable and necessary. In 1816 he wrote a letter to them, in which he explained how it would be more economical in the long run to have wheat ground and made into bread by the miller, rather than doing it at home.

'The best way, however, to satisfy your minds upon this subject is to suppose the same man to be both *Miller* and *Baker*, and to show you how much a *Load of Wheat* is sold for to the Miller, and how much it brings back from the public when paid for by them in the shape of bread. The distribution of the Load of Wheat stood thus:'

... and so Mr. Cobbett's calculations showed that the miller made only £8. 11s. 0d. profit on a load of wheat, and for this he provided all these services:

122

The tower mills built in the 15th century were an improvement on the post mills and because the body did not need to turn round, they had fixed towers. The 'cap' on the top carried the sails and the windshaft, and turned round in the wind. This is a small 18th century tower mill at Old Bolingbroke, Lincolnshire.

Smock mills are the newest of all and are a development of the tower mills. They are called 'smock' mills because they look like a 19th century farmer's smock. This smock mill is at Stelling-Minnis in Kent.

'The wheat to be put into the mill; beer for the carters; the grinding and dressing of the wheat; the sack to put the flour and offal into; the carrying of the flour and the offal; a delay in the sale; debts; the taxes on the Miller's horses, on all he uses and consumes.'

William Cobbett then listed the expenses of baking the bread. What do you think these might have been?

'Is it not wonderful that a load of wheat can be manufactured into bread and distributed at so *cheap* a rate?'

The earliest mills were watermills, and these have existed since Roman Britain. The Saxons built many mills, and the Domesday Book records about 5,000 in England.

Do you know what the Domesday Book was?

Almost every village which was near a stream must have had a mill.

Is there one left near your home? You can buy an Ordnance Survey map of your area, and old mills will be marked on this. You might not find a complete mill, but there will probably be some indication of where it stood.

The watermills worked by means of a sluice which controlled the water in the streams to provide enough power to drive the water wheel round.

The earliest windmills were built in the late twelfth century, in places where there was no water power, and usually in flat country, where there was plenty of wind to drive the sails. At one time there were as many as 10,000 mills at work in England. Today modern electric flour milling machinery provides all our flour. However, fortunately for us, the Windmill and Watermill Section of the Society for the Protection of Ancient Buildings has preserved a large number of mills which you can visit. They also try to encourage people to continue using the old milling machinery, and provide funds towards the cost of this.

You can become a member of the Society for the Protection of Ancient Buildings. And if you wish to visit some mills, they will

125

The Outwood Mill in Surrey is one of the few that are still working, and when you visit you can actually buy the flour that is ground there. This is the first floor of the mill, with the meal-bin on the left, and the centre post on the right.

These modern monsters now do the work of the old mills.

*send you a list of those which are open to the public, together
with opening times. At the Outwood Mill in Surrey you can
actually buy flour ground at the mill.*

The construction and repair of the mill was the work of the millwright. The millwright and his assistants had to be very strong to
manoeuvre the stocks of the sails into position, for they did not
have cranes to do the work, like engineers have today. The millwright also had to be a skilled and experienced craftsman to
construct the sails at the correct angles.

Museums to visit

If you would like to see some of the things you have read about in this book, these are some of the best places to visit.

Alton, Hampshire. The Curtis Museum.
A collection of Hampshire crafts and tools.
Bolton, Lancashire. Hall i'the Woods.
Former home of Samuel Crompton, inventor of the Spinning Mule.
Bristol. Blaise Castle House Museum.
Has a reconstructed corn-mill, and objects illustrating English life in former days.
Cambridge. Folk Museum.
Contains domestic and agricultural bygones and trade exhibits illustrating the life of the people of Cambridgeshire from mediaeval times.
Cardiff. National Museum of Wales.
Relics of trades and crafts.
Gloucester. Bishop Hooper's Lodging.

Collections illustrate bygone crafts and industries of the county.
Halifax. Bankfield Museum.
Textiles and machinery.
Halifax. West Yorkshire Folk Museum.
Coaches and harness; craft workshops.
Hull. Transport and Archaeological Museum.
Collection of coaches.
Kingussie. Highland Folk Museum.
Collection of Highland craft-work and tools.
Leeds. Abbey House Museum.
A folk museum illustrating the life and work of the people of Yorkshire over the last 300 years; it has three full-sized nineteenth-century streets of houses, shops and workplaces.
Leicester. Newarke House Museum.
Social history of the city from 1500 to the present day. History of the hosiery industry.
London. Bethnal Green Museum.
Spitalfields silks, porcelain and glass.
London. Geffrye Museum.
Display of period rooms showing the development of the English home from 1600. Display of cabinet maker's tools.
London. Horniman Museum.
Crafts from all over the world.
London. London Museum.
Domestic articles, swords, etc.—the growth of London and the life of its people from the Romans to the present day.
London. Science Museum.
Models of windmills, looms and spinning machinery, and other types of machines. Working models.
London. Victoria and Albert Museum.
Wrought-iron work, pottery.
Luton, Bedfordshire. Luton Museum and Art Gallery.
Rural trades and crafts, particularly straw crafts and pillow-lace.
Northampton. Abingdon Museum.
Folk material; period rooms.

Norwich. Bridewell Museum of Local Industries and Rural Crafts.
Local industries and crafts.

Reading. Museum of English Rural Life.
National collection of material about the history of the English
countryside. Housed in the University of Reading.

St Albans. City Museum.
Finest collection in Britain of craftsmen's tools.

St Fagan's, Glamorgan. Welsh Folk Museum.
Folk life exhibits, illustrating the social history of Wales.

Salisbury, Wiltshire. Salisbury and South Wiltshire Museum.
Local guild and craft relics.

Stroud, Gloucestershire. Stroud Museum.
Local crafts, and records of local mills.

York. Castle Museum.
Folk museum of Yorkshire life. Period rooms, crafts, and a water-
driven corn mill.

Acknowledgements

The author and publishers would like to thank the following individuals and organisations for permission to reproduce photographs. Every effort has been made to trace the owners of copyright material:

British Tourist Authority; Chrysler United Kingdom Limited; Miss Joyce Coleman; Council for Small Industries in Rural Areas; Council of Industrial Design; Daimler Company Limited; Miss Angela Gibson; Hereford City Library and Museums; The Mansell Collection; Ivan Martin, The Cricklade Pottery; Harry Meyer; National Coal Board; National Trade Union of Coopers; Radio Times Hulton Picture Library; Ridgeway Forge; Thomas Robinson & Sons Limited; The Science Museum; Thomas Smith Limited; Society for the Protection of Ancient Buildings; Josiah Wedgwood & Sons Limited; Wilkinson Sword Limited; Worshipful Company of Basketmakers; Worshipful Company of Weavers.

132

Index

133

coopers, 108–10, 116
coracles, 56
Coram, Thomas, 28
corn dollies, 84, 86, 88
Corn Law (1815), 122
Court of Pie Powder, 101
Court of the Exchequer, 100
Craft Guilds, 51–5
  admission to, 53–4
  and markets, 101
  of Basketmakers, 59
  of Blacksmiths, 40
  of Brewers, 72
  of Dyers, 54
  of Fishmongers, 55
  of Vintners, 54
  of Weavers, 51–2
Crompton, Samuel, 12

Daimler Motor Company, 98
Damocles, 41
Decorative Straw Work, 88
Dickens, Charles, 30, 92–3
Dionysius, 41
Doggett's Coat and Badge Race, 55
Domesday Book, 125
Dryden, John, 9
duelling, 49
Dumas, Alexandre, 49

East India Company, 43
Eastcheap, 102
Egbert, King of Wessex, 43
Egyptians, 56–7
Elizabeth I, Queen, 18, 81, 93, 102
Elizabeth II, Queen, 54, 98
Everyday Book, 103
Exchequer Roll, 52
exports, 9, 58–9

Factory Act (1802), 27
Factory Act (1819), 27
Farmer's Letters, 94–5
farriery, 36, 38
Feudal System, 34–5

Fiennes, Celia, 20
'Flying Coach', 93–4
Flying Shuttle, 12, 13
Foundling Hospital, 28
Freemen, 52
Frost Fairs, 102
fulling, 13, 16

Gauls, 45
General Strike (1926), 25
George I, King, 105
George III, King, 96
George VI, King, 43, 59
Goddess of Fertility, 86–8
'Golden Age' of coaching, 95
Golden Dolly, The, 88
Great Exhibition (1851), 63
Greeks, 64, 71

Hargreaves, James, 12
Harnett, Cynthia, 16
Harvest Festival, 86–8
Henry V, King, 72
Henry VIII, King, 84
Highway Code (1816), 92
Hiring Fairs, *see* Mop Fairs
Hone, William, 103
Hounslow Heath, 49
Howard, Katherine, 84

Industrial Revolution, 18, 54

James I, King, 49, 108

Kay, James, 12, 13
Kingsley, Charles, 28

Labour Party, 23
lace making, 81
Lambeth, M., 88
Lawrence, D.H., 19, 20
livery, 52
Livery Companies, *see* Craft Guilds
locksmiths, 36
Longfellow, 32, 36, 37

134

INDEX

135

Some other books to read

If you are interested in social history, and want to learn about other things as well as trades and crafts, the following books are very good.

A History of Everyday Things in England by Marjorie and C. M. B. Quennell, published by Batsford.
Vol. I: 1066-1499
Vol. II: 1500-1799
Vol. III: 1799-1851
Vol. IV: 1851-1914
Vol. V: 1914-1968

English Life Series, published by Batsford
Life in Medieval England by J. J. Bagley
Life in Elizabethan England by A. H. Dodd
Life in Georgian England by E. N. Williams
Life in Regency England by R. J. White

How they Lived Series, published by Basil Blackwell.